FIRST TIME RENTERS GUIDE

By KRISTENIA HARGROVE

All rights reserved. This book or parts thereof may not be reproduced in any form, stored in any retrieval system, or transmitted in any form by any means—electronic, mechanical, photocopy, recording, or otherwise—without prior written permission of the publisher, except as provided by United States o

America copyright law. For permission requests, write to the publisher, at "Attention: Permissions Coordinator," at the address below.

THE KOUTURE GROUP

Kouturerealtygroup@gmail.com

For information about special discounts available for bulk purchases, sales promotions, fund-raising, and educational needs, contact

THE KOTURE GROUP. Sales at Kouturerealtygroup@gmail.com

© 2022 The Kouture Group LLC. All rights reserved.

DEDICATION

This book is dedicated to my past, present and future clients, thank you for inspiring me!

Table of Contents

Acknowledgements 5

Chapter One-Chapter-Things To Consider Before Renting 6

Chapter Two- Location Location Location 8

Chapter Three-Credit Score 9

Chapter Four-Should I Hire A Realtor? 10

Chapter Five-Benefits of DIY (Doing It Yourself) 11

Chapter Six-The Application Process 12

Chapter Seven-Rejected Application…Now What? 16

Pro Tips 17

About The Author 18

Acknowledgements

CONGRATULATIONS! Moving into your own place is a very rewarding and exciting experience, I have found in my 7 plus years of doing real estate that many people want to rent an apartment, condo or home but do not know where to start or what is required to apply.

This book was created to help those like you who are ready to find their ideal rental. We will cover topics in the next few chapters that will provide you with the steps on how to go about renting an apartment.

Please note that I am a licensed Realtor in New Jersey so some qualifications and requirements may vary by state, I suggest doing research on your state laws regarding renting prior to your search.

Chapter One: Things to Consider Before Renting

There are three things you must consider before going out to look at apartments. You must consider **budget, credit score and location.** I will break down each one in this chapter.

A **budget** is an estimate of income and expenses for a set period of time, usually the time frame is a month. Knowing your monthly income is essential to determining how much you can spend.

Grab a pen and use the below outline to list all of your sources of income and the dollar amount each source generates for the month. The column labeled expenses should include all recurring monthly bills such as rent, utilities, subscriptions, phone. Internet, cable, food and transportation costs.

Once you have listed all of your expenses and income for the month, add each item up under its column and enter the total number for expenses and the total number of income. By doing this, you will see how much money you have coming in which will allow you to determine how much you can spend.

The rule of thumb when it comes to how much you should spend on rent is to **not exceed 30% of your annual gross income**, for example if you are making $50k annually, then your monthly rent should not exceed $1,600. Not everyone follows this rule of thumb but it is helpful when It comes to ensuring that you do not overspend and prevents you from biting off more than you can chew financially.

Monthly Budget Outline

Income	Expenses
Total	**Total**

*Tip: When looking at apartments, look at what is included in your rent and what fees are paid separately. Do not just look at the rental amount, it is important to factor in additional expenses associated with the rental as this will be your overall monthly fee.

Chapter Two Location Location Location

Where you will reside and call home is the most important decision you will have to make. The location in which you choose to live in can have a significant impact on your happiness, comfort, and to some extent even your health. The selection of a home or apartment should go well beyond financial considerations. It should include questions of proximity to schools, shopping, work, and transportation.

This would be a good time to think about what type of area you would like to live in, what amenities would you like and how much space is needed to accommodate your household.

When moving to a new area you should drive by that area at different times of the day to get a feel of what the neighborhood is really like

If you do this before applying to the rental, you will know if this location will be suitable or not.

Chapter Three Credit Score

Credit Score is a big factor when it comes to the application process. Your credit score will help the landlord determine if you are financially responsible and the likelihood of you paying your rent on time based on what your credit report reflects.

Using websites such as Credit Karma.com or ordering your Fico credit report before applying can help avoid any surprises.

A credit score of 600 and up is ideal but if you are still working on your credit then you are not completely disqualified as landlords look for other things such as income to debt ratio and collections.

Obtaining a co signor could help boost your chances of approval if credit is an issue. A co signor also known as a guarantor is a person who has a strong monthly income and credit score, this person will be responsible if you default on the rent so when considering this option, you must disclose this to that individual before they agree to apply with you.

Chapter Four Should I Hire a Realtor?

In this chapter we will look at the benefits of hiring a realtor for your apartment search, in the next chapter we will look at the benefits of conducting your search without working with a realtor.

Here are 3 benefits to working with a realtor

1. **Realtors have access to the multiple listing service also known as MLS**

The MLS is a compilation of rentals that are listed on the market. These listings are often only accessible to realtors and will provide more information on the apartment and fees associated with the listing such as broker fee, security deposit etc.

2. **Realtors Help Save time**

Searching for an apartment can seem like a full time job especially if it's your first apartment. A realtor can cut down time significantly once they know what you are looking for and then will narrow down properties that match your criteria and set up tours with the rentals that meet your needs.

3. **Realtors Can help you avoid being scammed**

Rental scams are currently on the rise according to FBI.com in 2021, 11,578 people reported losing $350,328,166 due to rental and real estate scams. An unknowing renter may be asked to pay fees before viewing the apartment – this is a red flag. Using a realtor will eliminate these kinds of risks because they will know how to find legitimate rentals.

Chapter Five - Benefits of DIY (Doing It Yourself)

Now that we know why hiring a real estate agent would be beneficial when searching for an apartment. Let's discuss some benefits of going at your search alone.

1. **You Can avoid extra fees**

Free rental websites like Zillow and Apartments.com can be useful when wanting to DIY your apartment search and will allow you to work directly with the landlord which will cut out the broker fee and save you money.

2. **Flexibility**

Most apartment complexes have an on-site property manager whose job includes giving prospective tenants tours of the property. So, it's easy to schedule a tour of the apartment on your own. You don't need the help of a real estate agent in this case. Book a tour directly with the landlord.

Chapter Six Application Process

Once you have decided to either hire a realtor or search on your own the next step is applying for the apartment. When applying some landlords require an application fee which will allow them to check your credit and background history, the application fees can range from $25-100. You will also be asked to provide income verification documents such as paystubs, tax returns and/or bank statements along with other information that we will go over in this chapter.

The first thing to is to fill out the rental application.

This application will be provided to you by the property manager or owner of the rental. If you have a co signor, roommate or anyone moving with you and contributing to the rent that is 18 years or older they will have to fill out an application as well.

A typical rental application requires the following information:

- photo ID
- name
- address
- phone number
- email
- employment and income information
- previous address
- pets (if applicable)
- emergency contacts
- background information
- landlord references
- personal or professional references (I suggest providing a minimum of 2)

2. Pay the apartment application fee

The application fee funds the credit and background checks done on potential renters. It essentially covers the screening cost of the applicant.

The rent application fee itself differs depending on various factors, such as the area, the building, or even the landlord.

Be sure to ask your potential landlord if any fees are refundable should they decide to go with another applicant.

4. Prove you can pay rent

An important part of the rental application process is providing proof of employment or income. Most landlords will ask for copies of tax returns, recent pay stubs or other forms of receipts from an employer.

Depending on your job, you may also provide recent bank statements, copies of client contracts, or copies of one or two W-2 forms if need be

Employment and credit checks usually take the longest, which is why most applications can take up to 72 hours. Rental application process time also varies depending on the property, so make sure to check with the landlord or property manager for the best estimate.

5. Figure out if you need a co-signer

The next step in the apartment application process is figuring out if you need a co-signer or not. A co-signer is a person with good credit who acts as a willing guarantor. If you have bad credit or insufficient credit history, they take the legal responsibility of paying your rent in case you won't.

Co-signers or guarantors may step in when first-time renters have no way of accounting for rental history or commitment to monthly rent and bill payments. You might need one in case your monthly income is less than two times the rent. You may also look at a co-signer as a way to strengthen your application and improve your chances of approval. Please be sure to notify the individual of the responsibility that they will take on if you default on rent before they agree to help you.

8. Pay Move in fees

This is when you discuss upfront costs like the security deposit and any additional fees. Deposit requirements are typically state-regulated. Most landlords will ask for the equivalent of one or one and a half months' rent in case you fall back on rent payments, so bring a certified bank check and ask for receipts. This is also the time for any last-minute questions you might have, such as how soon can you get the keys to the place, how rent will be paid to the landlord or should you bring your own refrigerator. **Please note that if you hired a realtor to find this rental, you may be responsible for the broker fee which will be due at move in, in addition to your security deposit. The broker fee is equal to one month rent.**

9. Sign the lease

You've passed the rental application process, inspected the premises, checked for parking space, made a quick note of the neighbors, and went through things to consider before renting now It's time to sign the lease!

It goes without saying that reading the lease agreement carefully is essential. Make sure you take your time to understand the details of your lease before planning your move-in date, such as what happens if you must break the lease in case of unexpected circumstances.

10. Get The Keys!

Time to call the moving trucks, pick out furniture and transfer the utilities that you have to pay into your name. You have successfully rented an apartment!

Chapter Seven Rejected Application……Now What?

News of a rejected application can be disheartening however it is not the end of the world. There are a few things that you can do when this happens.

1. Find out the reason for this decision, you should receive an adverse action letter that will detail the reason for the rejection.
2. Get a cosigner. A co signor is someone who will apply for the apartment with you and this person will have to submit an application and meet the income requirements.
3. Offer to pay at least 6-12 months in advance rent so that the landlord can feel comfortable knowing that your rent will be prepaid and this shows you are serious and responsible.
4. Take some time to work on the issues whether it be credit or income that got you the rejection decision. Do not lose hope and once the issues have been resolved, resume your search.

Chapter Eight PRO TIPS

1. Take pictures of the apartment before and after moving in.
2. Get renters insurance, this will protect your personal items in the event that there is a fire or flood. Keep in mind that the landlord's insurance policy only covers the building, not your stuff
3. Do not hold rent money, if the landlord has not made repairs in your apartment, put the rent money with the court until the landlord completes the repairs. I would advise seeking legal advice for the proper procedure.
4. Do a walkthrough before moving and be sure to address any repairs that need to be completed before you move into the apartment.

ABOUT THE AUTHOR

Kristenia Hargrove is a licensed realtor in the state of New Jersey and has been in the real estate industry since birth and has practiced for seven plus years and counting. Kristenia has won numerous awards for her success and exceptional customer service. When she is not renting apartments or selling homes, Kristenia enjoys spending time with her family and loves to travel.

THANK YOU FOR MAKING IT TO THE END OF THIS BOOK, I HOPE IT HELPS YOU ON YOUR APARTMENT SEARCH JOURNEY.

IF YOU OR SOMEONE YOU KNOW NEEDS ASSISTANCE WITH BUYING, SELLING OR RENTING A HOME, EMAIL US AT KOUTUREREALTYGROUP@GMAIL.COM

© 2022 The Kouture Group LLC. All rights reserved.

www.ingramcontent.com/pod-product-compliance
Lightning Source LLC
Chambersburg PA
CBHW081529240526
45465CB00029B/2808